Alexander Graham Bell

by Emily James

Pebble® Plus

raintree

a Capstone company — publishers for children

Raintree is an imprint of Capstone Global Library Limited, a company incorporated in England and Wales having its registered office at 264 Banbury Road, Oxford, OX2 7DY – Registered company number: 6695582

www.raintree.co.uk
myorders@raintree.co.uk

Editorial Credits
Jaclyn Jaycox and Michelle Hasselius, editors; Jennifer Bergstrom, designer; Jo Miller, media researcher; Steve Walker, production specialist

ISBN 978 1 474 7 3444 8
21 20 19 18 17
10 9 8 7 6 5 4 3 2 1

British Library Cataloguing in Publication Data
A full catalogue record for this book is available from the British Library.

Acknowledgements
We would like to thank the following for permission to reproduce images: Alamy: Pictorial Press, 17; Getty Images: Archive Photos/Smith Collection/Gado, 7, Bettmann, 13, National Geographic/Dr. Gilbert H. Grosvenor, 15, The LIFE Picture Collection/Mansell/Time Life Pictures, 11; Newscom: Ken Welsh, 19, ZUMA Press/JT Vintage, cover, 1, 21; Science Source, 9; Wikimedia: Kim Traynor, 5
Design Elements: Shutterstock: aliraspberry, Charts and BG, mangpor2004, Ron and Joe, sumkinn, Yurii Andreichyn

Every effort has been made to contact copyright holders of material reproduced in this book. Any omissions will be rectified in subsequent printings if notice is given to the publisher.

All the internet addresses (URLs) given in this book were valid at the time of going to press. However, due to the dynamic nature of the internet, some addresses may have changed, or sites may have changed or ceased to exist since publication. While the author and publisher regret any inconvenience this may cause readers, no responsibility for any such changes can be accepted by either the author or the publisher.

Printed and bound in China.

Contents

FAMILY

Alexander Graham Bell was born in Edinburgh, Scotland in 1847. His father was a teacher who taught people how to speak clearly.

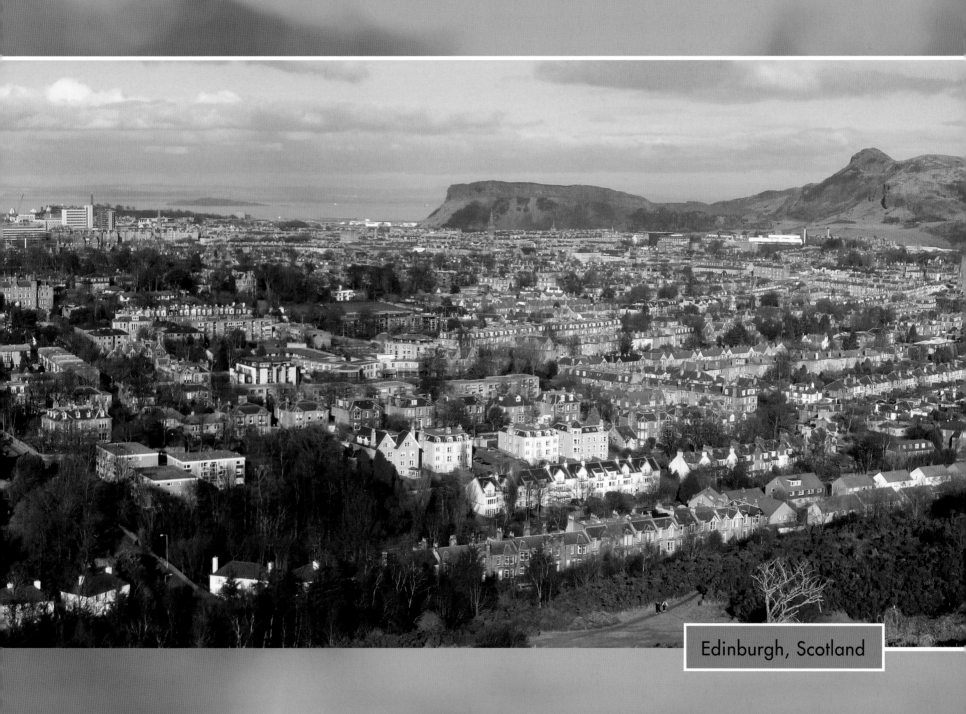

Edinburgh, Scotland

Alexander's mother was deaf.
But she was a gifted pianist.
She taught him how to play
the piano. Alexander was
good at music and science.

Alexander
Graham Bell

Alexander with his mother,
father and brothers in 1870

EARLY YEARS

Alexander was interested in

sound and how it travels.

He also liked to invent things.

Alexander built his first invention

when he was 12 years old.

Alexander at age 14 or 15

In 1871 Alexander moved
to Boston, Massachusetts, USA.
He taught deaf students how
to communicate. He also
experimented with sound.

Alexander Graham Bell

Alexander and his students at Boston School for the Deaf in 1871

Alexander wanted to learn about electricity. In 1874 he met Tom Watson. Tom knew how electricity worked.

Alexander Graham Bell (left) and Tom Watson

INVENTING THE TELEPHONE

Alexander stopped teaching.

He and Tom wanted to invent

a machine. They hoped

it would send voices from

one place to another.

Alexander Graham Bell

Alexander testing an invention that collects moisture

15

On 10 March 1876 Alexander
and Tom reached their goal.
They invented the first telephone.
The two men spoke to each
other through the machine.

The first words Alexander said on the telephone were, "Mr. Watson, come here. I want you."

LATER YEARS

Alexander and Tom made their telephone better. Soon it could send voices over many miles. In 1915 they made the first telephone call across the United States.

Alexander at the opening of the long-distance telephone line from New York to Chicago in 1892

Alexander died in 1922

as a respected teacher and

inventor. His work had changed

the way people communicate

with each other.

Alexander in 1920

Glossary

communicate pass along thoughts, feelings or information

deaf unable to hear

electricity natural force that can be used to make light and heat or to make machines work

experiment scientific test to find out how something works

invent think up and make something new

pianist someone who plays the piano

respect have a high opinion of someone

Read more

Alexander Graham Bell (Science Biographies), Catherine Chambers (Raintree, 2014)

Alexander Graham Bell, Barbara Kramer (National Geographic, 2015)

The First Telephone: Alexander Graham Bell's Amazing Invention, Catherine Chambers (DK Publishing, 2015)

Websites

www.sciencekids.co.nz/sciencefacts/scientists/
alexandergrahambell.html
Learn fun information about the inventor of the telephone.

www.biography.com/news/alexander-graham-bell-biography-
facts
Discover fun facts about Alexander Graham Bell.

Comprehension questions

1. What did Alexander's mother teach him to do when he was a child?

2. Alexander liked to invent things. What does "invent" mean?

3. Imagine you are Alexander on 10 March 1876. You are about to make the first telephone call. What would you say?

Index